Elizabeth Sedgwick Vaill

An American's Patriotic Catechism

Elizabeth Sedgwick Vaill

An American's Patriotic Catechism

ISBN/EAN: 9783743686892

Printed in Europe, USA, Canada, Australia, Japan

Cover: Foto ©Lupo / pixelio.de

More available books at **www.hansebooks.com**

·AN AMERICAN'S
PATRIOTIC . CATECHISM

A Brief History of the Settlement
of the American Colonies, Their
Royal Charters, the Causes of Their
Separation, and the Establishment
of Their Independence of Great
Britain, in the form of Question
and Answer. -   -   -   -   -

By ELIZABETH SEDGWICK VAILL.

NEW YORK:
THE REPUBLIC PRESS
1896

PREFACE.

" Who, with heart and eyes, could walk
Where Liberty had been,—nor see
The shining foot-prints of her Deity ?"

THIS LITTLE BOOK has been prepared with an
imaginary audience of those who love the
story of Liberty attained by our forefathers.
If the answers to the questions do not satisfy,
my end as compiler will be gained if they
lead to a careful study of our Country's History
as told by Bancroft, Lossing, Fiske and others.
It has been my aim to connect the story so as
to make each month or year the father of the
next. I shall be glad if " children of a larger
growth " find their memories refreshed as to
dates of important events. The time has gone
by when one can sit by the fireside and listen
to the recitals of a grandfather who, becoming
fired with his theme, "shoulders his crutch,
and shows how fields were won." But the time
has not come when we can afford to forget
that the Country of which we, as Americans, are
so proud, has cost the lives and fortunes of our
ancestors. Let us cherish, then, that Liberty so
dearly bought.

E. S. V.

DEMAREST, N. J., December, 1896.

Ans. In 1583, by Sir Walter Raleigh, half-brother of Sir Humphrey Gilbert, the former having obtained a transfer of the latter's patent.

3. What did this charter to Sir Walter include ?

Ans. Nearly all the land on the Atlantic coast now called the United States.

4. Was the expedition sent out by Raleigh successful ?

Ans. The only thing accomplished was the naming of nearly all the eastern coast Virginia in honor of the Queen, and the introduction of tobacco into England.

5. When was the first permanent English settlement made ?

Ans. In 1607, under James I., who had given charters to two companies, called " The London Company " and " The Plymouth Company."

6. Which company made the first settlement ?

Ans. The London Company, which sent out three ships and one hundred and five men, under Capt. Christopher Newport.

7. Where did they land ?

Ans. They were driven by storms into Chesapeake Bay, from which they ascended a river which they named for King James. Proceeding about forty miles up the river, they landed, built a few huts, and named the place Jamestown.

8. By whom was the next settlement made ?

Ans. By the Plymouth Company, which sent out a party of one hundred persons in the ship " Mayflower."

9. Where did they land ?

Ans. Inside of Cape Cod, on the shore of what had been called "New England," by Capt. John Smith, as early as 1614. The rock on which they landed was called " Plymouth Rock," after the Plymouth Company.

10. What was the date of this landing ?

Ans. December 21st (new style), 1620.

11. What name has been given to those who came over in the Mayflower ?

Ans. "The Pilgrim Fathers."

12. What names were given to the two colonies ?

Ans. The London Company's settlement was called " Virginia," and that of the Plymouth Company was called " Massachusetts."

13. How were the rest of the thirteen English colonies formed ?

Ans. Principally from Virginia and Massachusetts; but also by companies direct from England.

PART II.

ROYAL CHARTERS.

14. When, and under what Sovereign, did each colony receive its Royal Charter?

Ans. (i) VIRGINIA's liberal charter, received by the London Company in 1607, had enabled her to flourish as a colony; but James I., jealous of her growing power, in 1624 annulled this charter. Before he had completed a new code of laws for the Province, he died, and his son, Charles I., succeeded him. After many years of strife, and even extreme distress, under the governors sent from England, Virginia again became a royal province under Charles II., 1684.

(ii) MASSACHUSETTS, whose pioneers landed on Plymouth Rock in 1620, conformed to the Plymouth Company's grant. Large accessions to this Colony were soon made by those who sought religious freedom in the wilds of New England, and, in 1629, they received from Charles I. a charter confirming that of the Plymouth Company, and conveying to them powers of government. They were called "The Massachusetts Bay Colony."

(iii) In NEW HAMPSHIRE settlements were made on the Piscataqua river in 1623. It became a distinct Royal Province in 1680 under Charles II.

(iv) RHODE ISLAND was settled in 1636 by Roger Williams, who had been driven from Massachusetts on account of his religious opinions. He obtained a grant of land from Canonicus, chief Sachem of the Narragansetts, and in recognition of "God's merciful providence in his distress," he called the place Providence. He obtained a free charter in 1644.

(v) CONNECTICUT was first settled by the Dutch at Hartford. They gave way to several English Colonies, who combined under one name in 1636 under a charter from Charles I.

(vi) NEW YORK was first settled by the Dutch in 1614, but it was surrendered to the English in 1664 under Charles II.

(vii) NEW JERSEY was settled by the Dutch in 1620. The first permanent English settlement was at Elizabethtown in 1664. She became a separate Royal Province in 1736 under George II.

(viii) PENNSYLVANIA was settled in 1681 by William Penn, who obtained a grant of territory from Charles II.

(ix) DELAWARE was first settled by the Dutch,

Swedes, and Finns, but was taken by the English in 1664 and became an English Colony under Queen Anne in 1703.

(x) MARYLAND's first English settlement was made by Lord Baltimore at St. Mary's, under a special charter from Charles I. in 1632.

(xi) NORTH CAROLINA was settled in 1663 by a company of English noblemen to whom Charles II. had granted the territory between Virginia and Florida. This grant reverted to the Crown in 1729, when North Carolina became, under George II., a distinct Royal Province.

(xii) SOUTH CAROLINA, settled by the English in 1670, obtained her separate charter in 1729 under George II.

(xiii) GEORGIA was settled in 1733 by an English gentleman (General James Oglethorpe), who made a settlement at Savannah and named the province Georgia, after George II.

PART III.

CAUSES LEADING TO THE WAR OF THE REVOLUTION.

15. Did the inhabitants of the thirteen Colonies live contentedly under English government?

Ans. No; they suffered many acts of tyranny and oppression.

16. Mention seven of the earlier causes of dissatisfaction with England?

Ans. (i) All laws regulating trade between the Colonies, and between the Colonies and other countries, were made by the English Parliament.

(ii) The Colonies were forced to send nearly all their leading products to England for sale.

(iii) The Colonies were not allowed to buy European goods, except in England.

(iv) American manufactures were prohibited, and it was declared that the Colonists had no right to make a "horseshoe nail" without permission of Parliament.

(v) A "Navigation Act" was passed in 1660, which declared: "No merchandise shall be imported into the plantations but in English vessels, navigated by Englishmen, under penalty of forfeiture." Thus, foreign ships were prevented from entering any port of the Colonies.

(vi) Customs-houses were established in all principal ports, and duties were there collected for the King.

(vii) "Writs of Assistance" were given to English officers, conferring the right to search all places of business and private houses for smuggled goods.

17. How long had these wrongs existed ?

Ans. For more than one hundred years.

18. What act of injustice caused greater discontent than those just mentioned ?

Ans. An attempt to tax the Colonies to pay the expenses of a war between France and England, which closed in 1763.

19. What was the occasion of this war between France and England ?

Ans. The French had been fast gaining a foothold in America, and the English denied them the right.

20. Had the Colonies assisted England in this war ?

Ans. Yes; they had lost 30,000 men and spent $16,000,000, of which England had repaid only $5,000,000.

21. Why did the Colonies object to this tax ?

Ans. Because they had no representation in

Parliament, and they declared that "taxation without representation" was tyranny.

22. What was the form of this tax ?

Ans. It was called the "Stamp Act," and provided that a stamp bought of the English Government should be placed upon "all legal documents, newspapers, pamphlets, bills of lading, marriage certificates, wills, college diplomas, leases," etc.

23. Was any objection to this tax raised in Parliament.

Ans. William · Pitt, Edmund Burke, Isaac Barré, and others made eloquent and cogent appeals against this tax, as an act of oppression.

24. When did the Stamp Act become a law?

Ans. It was passed March 22, 1765, to go into effect the first of the following November. An attempt was made to have those who resisted sent to England for trial.

25. Was the Stamp Act enforced?

Ans. No. The Colonists made such resistance that no officer of the English government dared, or could, sell a stamp.

26. What were some of these acts of resistance ?

Ans. (i) A "Bill of Rights" was drawn up asserting that the Colonists were entitled to all the rights and privileges of natural born subjects of Great Britain.

(ii) Though America had almost no manu-factories, the merchants pledged themselves to import no English goods until the Stamp Act was repealed.

(iii) Boston said, "We will form a combina-tion to eat nothing, drink nothing and wear nothing imported from Great Britain."

(iv) When the day arrived for the Act to go into effect, muffled bells were tolled, flags were displayed at half-mast, Liberty was represented as dead by burial scenes, and Government stamp agents were hung in effigy.

27. What was the effect of these demonstra-tions ?

Ans. Parliament was obliged to consider the question of repeal.

28. What illustrious American was called before Parliament to give his opinion in regard to this tax ?

Ans. Benjamin Franklin, who was in Eng-land to urge a petition for the Pennsylvania Colony.

29. When did Franklin appear before Parlia-ment ?

Ans. February 13, 1766.

30. What impression did Franklin make in Parliament ?

Ans. His manly bearing and his wise and

brave answers gained him honor, and were without doubt the immediate cause of the repeal of the Stamp Act.

31. When was the Stamp Act repealed ?

Ans. March 18, 1766.

32. What was the next act of oppression by Parliament ?

Ans. In order to maintain the right of the English Government to tax the Colonies, new duties were imposed in 1767 on " glass, paper, painters' colors, tea, etc.," and a " Board of Trade," to act independently of the Colonies, was established at Boston.

33. How did Parliament now guard against any resistance on the part of the Colonies ?

Ans. Troops were sent to America to enforce these taxes, and by a " Mutiny Act," it was ordered that the Colonists should furnish these troops with quarters and supplies.

34. What was the effect of this Act upon the Colonists ?

Ans. They were filled with indignation at having to feed and shelter their oppressors. Frequent quarrels arose between the people and the soldiers, and on March 5, 1770, a fight resulted, in which eight inhabitants of Boston were killed and several wounded. This fight was called the " Boston Massacre."

35. How did Parliament receive the news of the resistance?

Ans. It took off all taxes except on tea, which was left to maintain the principle of the right of taxation.

36. How did the Colonists receive this concession?

Ans. As they, too, were contending for a principle, they refused to buy tea, and began to use as a substitute, raspberry leaves, sassafras, etc.

37. What was done with the tea sent from England?

Ans. Ships reaching New York and Philadelphia were sent back. At Boston, the British authorities would not allow the tea-ships to return.

38. In consequence what happened at Boston?

Ans. On the night of December 16, 1773, sixty men disguised as Indians boarded the ships, and emptied 342 chests of tea into Boston Harbor. This is known as the "Boston Tea-Party."

39. What action did the English Parliament then take?

Ans. On March 7, 1774, it passed a bill declaring the port of Boston closed until the tea destroyed should be paid for.

40. What was the effect of the Boston Port Bill on other Colonies?

Ans. (i) Letters of sympathy and material aid were sent to Boston, and assemblies protested against this measure.

(ii) Party lines were drawn, those opposed to Royalty being called Whigs and those in favor called Tories.

(iii) The brig "Peggy Stewart" arrived at Annapolis from London, October, 1774, with more than 2,000 lbs. of tea, on which the owner made haste to pay the duty. The people of Maryland resented this voluntary submission to the British claim, and kept a watch to prevent its landing until the two importers and the shipowner offered to burn the tea. This did not satisfy the people, and the owner of the brig then proposed to burn the brig also. This offer being accepted, the owner and importers went on board with hats off and lighted torches in their hands and set fire to the chests of tea, all of which, with every appurtenance of the "Peggy Stewart," was consumed. This is only one instance of the feeling that had been roused throughout the Colonies.

41. By what method did the Colonies express their UNITED sentiment?

Ans. By calling the First Continental Congress, which met at Philadelphia on Sept. 5, 1774.

42. What action did the Continental Congress take ?

Ans. It sustained Massachusetts in her resistance ; issued a protest against standing armies being kept in the Colonies without the consent of the people ; and agreed to hold no intercourse with Great Britain.

43. At what cost did the Colonists maintain their rights ?

Ans. As manufactures had been discouraged by England, the Colonists suffered many privations, until they learned to be self-reliant and produce their own necessaries of life.

44. What other act immediately followed the Boston Port Bill ?

Ans. The Quebec Act, which was a plan to subvert the charters of Massachusetts and other Colonies by taking away their dearest rights, and extending the boundaries of the "new government of Quebec" to the Ohio and the Mississippi, and over a region which included the area of the present States of Ohio, Michigan, Indiana, Illinois, and Wisconsin.

45. What sentiment was now growing in the minds of the Colonists ?

Ans. Before the year 1774 very few of the Colonists contemplated a separation from the Mother Country, but developments in the spring of that year aroused this very feeling.

PART IV.

THE COLONIES DECLARE, AND TAKE MEASURES, FOR INDEPENDENCE.

46. Where and when was the first united sentiment expressed that led to a separation from the Mother Country?

Ans. At the First Continental Congress, which met at Philadelphia, Sept. 5, 1774. The Declaration and Resolves then framed not only expressed the will of the Colonists, but paved the way for the Declaration of Independence.

47. What steps did this Congress take toward a reconciliation with the British government?

Ans. It petitioned the King in the most affectionate and respectful manner to restore the violated rights of the Colonists, as "English freemen."

48. While this First Continental Congress was thus in session at Philadelphia, what were English officers doing in New England?

Ans. They were seizing all military stores possible, and the Colonists were resisting and preparing for the conflict, now inevitable.

49. What were some of the first signs that war was imminent?

Ans. (i) The Second Provincial Congress of Massachusetts met in February, 1775, and appointed eleven men as their Committee of Safety, charged to resist every attempt at executing the acts of Parliament.

(ii) This committee was empowered to take possession of all warlike stores in the province, and to make returns of Militia and Minute-men who had been preparing for the conflict.

(iii) Work or supplies for the English troops were forbidden, and the committee was urged to prepare military stores and review the companies of Minute-men.

50. When did the Colonists first forcibly resist the English government?

Ans. On February 26, 1775, General Gage, who was the English officer in charge at Boston, having learned that a number of field-pieces were collected at Salem, sent a party of soldiers to take possession of them in the name of the King. The people of Salem, having been apprised of their approach, raised their drawbridge, and thus prevented their entering the town, and defeated their purpose.

51. When and where did the War of the Revolution actually begin?

Ans. On April 19, 1775, at Lexington and Concord, about sixteen miles from Boston.

52. What movement on the part of the British led to this collision?

Ans. The vigilant Dr. Joseph Warren, had discovered preparations by the British to take military stores which had been gathered at Concord.

53. What measures were taken to defeat this movement?

Ans. On the night of April 18th, Paul Revere, who also had watched developments, learned that British troops were to start about midnight for Concord, and that orders had been given to British sentinels to allow no one to leave the town. A few minutes before this order went into effect, Revere—having arranged for a friend to give the "lantern signals" now so memorable,—was rowed across the river Charles. The signals from the "Old North Church" being given, he mounted a horse that was in waiting, and struck out for the country beyond. A knock on the doors and a cry of alarm as he rushed through the towns and village streets, roused the inhabitants, and as the British troops advanced, the firing of guns and ringing of bells revealed that some herald had preceded them and warned the people of their approach. When the morning of April 19th dawned, Lexington

Green was alive with Minute-men, patriots from twenty-three towns having answered this "midnight call of Paul Revere." As the morning broke, Major Pitcairn under orders from Gage, leading 800 British soldiers, advanced, and when within a few rods of the American patriots cried out, "Disperse, ye rebels; lay down your arms!" "Too few to resist, too brave to fly," the Minute-men stood firm. Pitcairn then ordered his men to fire. The fire was feebly returned, and no harm was done to the British troops; but Lexington lost seven men killed and nine wounded. Then the British troops drew up on the green, fired a volley, huzzaed three times in triumph, and after a short halt marched on to Concord.

54. What did they accomplish at Concord?

Ans. They found nothing in the way of military stores worthy the name; for the guns had been spiked and other material removed.

55. How did the troops show their chagrin at this failure?

Ans. Angry at this fruitless march, they burned the liberty pole, set fire to the courthouse and rifled private dwellings.

56. Was any blood shed at Concord?

Ans. Yes. The Minute-men, having heard of the fight at Lexington, gathered and marched to meet the British. On nearing the Concord river, to prevent the Minute-men from crossing the British began to take up the planks of the bridge. Finding the Americans resolute, a skirmish occurred. Three patriots were killed, and the British lost two men. The British then retreated in disorder, leaving the countrymen in possession of the bridge.

57. How many were killed and wounded in this raid ?

Ans. The British were terribly assailed all the way on their retreat, and when on the morning of April 20th, they crossed over to Boston, their loss was ascertained to be in killed and wounded 273. The American loss was less than 100.

58. What important military move did the Americans then make ?

Ans. They began blockading Boston, and very soon many thousands of men from New Hampshire, Rhode Island and Connecticut were at work with the Massachusetts men building intrenchments to shut in the British. The swift response from other Colonies showed how strong the determination was to avenge the shedding of innocent blood, and also, that a firm conviction had at last seized the people, that liberty must come at all hazards.

59. What was the immediate result of the blockade?

Ans. This sudden stoppage of supplies of all kinds caused much suffering to the troops and residents.

60. What partial relief did Gage institute?

Ans. He allowed the patriots in the city, men, women, and children, a safe conduct out of the town, upon condition that they would not join in any attack upon the troops, leave all their arms and ammunition in Faneuil Hall, and take no provisions. He soon rescinded this order, however, leaving many thousands of people still in the city.

61. What was the immediate effect of the "news from Lexington" upon other Colonies?

Ans. (i) On the 23d of April, New York, filled with indignation, declared her allegiance to England null and void. Sloops lying at her wharves laden with supplies, to the value of eighty thousand pounds, for British troops at Boston, were unloaded. On following days the military stores of the city were secured, volunteer companies paraded the streets, and on May 1, 1775, at the usual time and places of election, a new Committee of One Hundred men was chosen, which resolved, in the most explicit manner, to "stand or fall with the Liberty of the Continent."

(ii) New Jersey patriots were willing to hazard their lives and fortunes in support of Massachusetts.

(iii) Pennsylvania said, "Let us not be bold in declaration and cold in action."

(iv) Maryland gave up the arms and ammunition of the province to their "freemen."

(v) Virginia, on the 2d of May, at the "cry from Lexington," signified her readiness to obey the call for Liberty.

(vi) North and South Carolina proceeded to place their Colonies in a state of defence.

(vii) The skirmish at Lexington having become known in Savannah on the 10th of May, Georgia joined the Union and sent 63 barrels of rice and 122 pounds in spices to the "Boston Wanderers."

62. What military step of great importance did the Americans next take?

Ans. They captured Fort Ticonderoga and Crown Point, where a large number of cannon and other military stores were held by the British. Connecticut, acting on her own responsibility, with Col. Ethan Allen of her own Colony at the head of eighty backwoodsmen, principally from the New Hampshire grants (now Vermont) made a sudden descent upon Ticonderoga on the early morning of May 10,

1775, and demanded its surrender. The officer in charge inquired, "By whose authority?" Colonel Allen responded, "In the name of the Great Jehovah and the Continental Congress." The demand was immediately complied with, and Ticonderoga, that had cost England eight million pounds sterling and many lives, was won in ten minutes by a few undisciplined men, without the loss of life or limb. More than one hundred brass cannon and many small stores were taken, which were of great service to the future Continental Army. Ticonderoga and Crown Point, which latter was captured at the same time by Col. Seth Warner, were both near the head of Lake Champlain and on the high road to Canada.

63. What civil measures were the Colonists now taking?

Ans. The "Second Continental Congress" was assembling at Philadelphia. The Colonies now numbering 3,000,000 people had begun to realize their importance and their power. They also began to see that Liberty in its best form must be assumed and maintained, and the assembling of this Second Congress on May 10, 1775, was at the call of the Colonies.

64. What work lay before the Congress?

Ans. No power was intrusted to it save that

of counsel, and it represented only the unformed opinions of an unformed people.

65. What was its first important action?

Ans. After much conference with the Colonies, and while news of encounters and engagements were constantly coming to them, a Gen-
eralissimo was asked for, to educate and form
the rude forces which had been for a month or
more gathering around Boston.   In answer to
this demand on June 15, 1775, at the particu-
lar request of New England, George Washington of Virginia, a member of the Continental
Congress, was nominated, and by ballot unanimously elected as '' Commander-in-Chief.''

66. Meanwhile, what other significant engagements, besides the taking of Fort Ticonderoga, occurred in May of 1775?

Ans. When the intelligence of the conflict at
Lexington and Concord reached the port of
Machias, in the Maine district, the people determined to seize the '' Margretta '' and her con-
voy, lying in port loading with lumber for the
British at Boston.   The officer in charge, discovering the hostile intent of the people,
weighed anchor, and moved down the river to a
wharf about four miles below the town.   Not to
be thwarted, a few young men seized a timber
sloop lying at the wharf, secured the captain

and crew, called for volunteers, and with twenty fowling pieces, thirteen pitchforks, a dozen narrow axes, a few pounds of pork, a bag of bread, and a barrel of water, they set sail with a fair breeze from the northwest. The sloop proved to be the better sailer, and the schooner was speedily overtaken. The "Margretta" fired upon the sloop, but the fire was returned with good effect. The Britisher was boarded; Joseph Wheaton of the sloop lowered the schooner's colors, and thus ended the first naval victory of the United Colonies. The "Margretta" was manned by two commissioned officers and thirty-eight warrant and petty officers. She carried an ample supply of powder and ball, ten six pounders, twenty swivels, forty muskets, forty cutlasses, forty picks, forty boarding axes, ten pairs of pistols, etc. The exact loss of life on either side has not been recorded, but the aggregate did not exceed twenty. This first blow struck on the water after the war of the Revolution had actually begun, has been called the "Lexington of the Sea," for it was characterized by a rising of the people against a regular force, a long chase, a bloody struggle and a triumph.

67. Mention other encounters in May, 1775?

Ans. Boston was so beleaguered, that the only

supplies possible for the British army must be obtained from islands in or near the harbor. On the 21st of May an attempt to get the hay on Grape Island was discovered about sunrise. Alarm guns were fired, drums beat to arms, bells were rung, and patriots at once secured boats and pushed off; but the English retreated, and the Americans set fire to the hay. On the 27th an attempt was made to secure or destroy hay and stock on Noddle's and Hog Islands, lest it should prove an aid to the British. A schooner and sloop, sent from the British squadron to prevent this, were forced to give up their purpose, with the loss by the English of twenty killed and fifty wounded, and by the provincials of four slightly wounded.

68. What famous battle occurred June 17, 1775?

Ans. The Battle of Bunker Hill. This battle has been the theme of the home and the fireside more often, perhaps, than that of any other engagement.

69. What led directly to this battle?

Ans. The Colonists had learned that the British intended to fortify Bunker Hill, and they determined to anticipate them. George Washington, who was elected Commander-in-Chief of the Army on June 15th, had not as yet assumed command. A body of about 1,500 Americans, under Capt. William Prescott, assembled at Cambridge on June 16th, and, under cover of the night, they marched to the place appointed. When the morning of the 17th dawned, the British were startled by the view of a redoubt on the Hill, that had not been seen before. Resolved to drive the Americans from the position thus occupied during the night, General Howe crossed the Charles river with 3,000 men, and, forming at the landing, they slowly ascended the Hill. The patriot ranks lay quietly behind the breastworks until the British were within ten rods, when, at a command from Prescott, a blaze of light shot from the redoubt, and whole platoons of British fell. There was a second advance, with a like result. At a third advance, only one volley smote them, for the ammunition of the Americans was exhausted. The British then charged, with fixed bayonets, and though the patriots resisted with clubbed muskets, they were driven from the field. The British were too much broken to pursue, and the effect upon the Americans of this first regular battle of the Revolution was that of victory. The British lost in killed and wounded about 1,100, and the Americans about 400. The one great loss to the Colonists was that of the brave Gen. Joseph Warren, who was one of America's truest sons. When the tidings of the Battle of Charlestown (Bunker Hill) reached the Continental Congress, Patrick Henry exclaimed: "A breach on our affection was needed to rouse the country to action."

70. When and where did Washington take command of the American Army?

Ans. At Cambridge, on July 3, 1775. Soon after his appointment he left Philadelphia for New England. Congress had adopted the undisciplined troops around Boston as the "Continental Army," and appointed general officers to assist Washington in its organization and future operations.

71. What was Washington's first step on assuming command?

Ans. To make returns to Congress of the condition of affairs at Boston.

72. What was the apparent situation of the British forces?

Ans. From Prospect Hill, in Cambridge, Washington took a view of Boston and Charlestown. The latter town having been burned, nothing was to be seen of it but ruins of the former homes of patriots. Above these ruins rose the tents of the British, who were strongly posted on Bunker Hill, and their sentries were extended one hundred and fifty yards beyond Charlestown Neck. On Breed's Hill, Copp's Hill, and other important points, men with batteries were on guard. A twenty-gun ship was anchored below Charlestown ferry, and three floating batteries lay on the Mystic. The Light Horse and a few men were in Boston. The remainder were on Roxbury Neck, strongly fortified with outposts so far advanced that the sentries of the two armies could almost have conversation with each other. Of the inhabitants of Boston, nearly 7,000 still remained in town. These were confined to their homes after ten o'clock at night, deprived of wholesome food, liable to be robbed without redress, and exposed to the malice of the British soldiery.

73. How was the American Army disposed?

Ans. They were gathered in a semicircle, from the west end of Dorchester to Malden, a distance of twelve miles. Entrenchments had been thrown up at convenient places. The main street at Roxbury was defended by a breastwork, in front of which sharpened trees pointing toward Boston prevented the approach of Light Horse, and sentinels and smaller posts stretched beyond the Malden river.

74. What was the size of the American Army at this time ?

Ans. The American rolls recorded 17,000 men, but Washington never had more than 14,500 fit for duty. To bring all these crude volunteers into working order and fortify every weak point was the imperative need, but "Washington's strong and uniform will was exerted with a quiet and commanding energy."

75. What acts of the army occurred in July, 1775?

Ans. Skirmishes between the Americans and the British were frequent. On July 8th, the British advance guard nearest Roxbury was driven in and several muskets taken. On the night of the 10th, 300 American Volunteers swept Long Island, in Boston Harbor, of a large number of sheep and cattle, and took sixteen prisoners. Two days later, an American officer with a number of men went to the same island and burned the hay which was stacked there for the British cavalry. Other American companies went to Weymouth and Hingham, and reaped and brought off the ripe grain from Nantasket. On the night of the 20th, Vose, a Major in Heath's regiment, set fire to the lighthouse in Boston Harbor, and brought off ammunition and lamps.

His party was pursued by a British man-of-war, but the adventurous soldiers escaped. Carpenters, with a guard of thirty British marines, were sent to repair the lighthouse; but on the 30th they were attacked by a party of Americans from Dorchester and Squantum, who killed the lieutenant and one man and captured all the rest of the party: The Americans had one killed and two or three wounded. On the next day, in "general orders," Washington praised their gallant and soldier-like conduct.

76. By what means was the Continental Army supplied with the necessaries of life?

Ans. Through the thoughtful benevolence and patriotism of the Massachusetts Colony. Each householder deemed himself a sort of commissary. Such articles as could be spared were devoted to the camp, and everybody's wagons were used to forward them. The troops were fed by the unselfish care of the people, without so much as a barrel of flour from Congress.

77. What was Congress waiting for?

Ans. It still had hopes that its repeated appeals to King George would result in conciliatory measures.

78. What was accomplished by the Americans in August, 1775.

Ans. By the 4th of that month the army was formed into three grand divisions: at Roxbury, Cambridge and Winter Hill.

79. Who commanded these divisions?

Ans. Generals Artemas Ward, Charles Lee, and Israel Putnam.

80. What special work was being done by them?

Ans. With these forces, Washington was closely investing Boston.

81. What movement was made in regard to Canada?

Ans. To prevent Canada being a place of rendezvous and supplies· for Great Britain, a committee went to Cambridge to consult with Washington.

82. What was the result of this conference?

Ans. The commandants at Fort Ticonderoga and Crown Point were directed to proceed by way of Lake Champlain to Montreal and Quebec. On August 31st, Gen. Richard Montgomery left Crown Point for the purpose of of invading Canada, and was joined by Philip Schuyler on September 4th. General Washington also sent an expedition, under Col. Benedict Arnold, by way of the Kennebec and Chaudiere rivers, to attack Quebec.

83. What was effected by these expeditions?

Ans. On reaching Canada, Montgomery proceeded down the Sorrel River to St. John, where there was a strong British garrison. The fort was besieged, but made an obstinate resistance till November 3, 1775, when it was taken. Montgomery then pressed on to Montreal, which was taken on November 13th. Reaching on toward Quebec, Montgomery was met before that citadel by Colonel Arnold, who had taken an eastern route, by way of Kennebec river. Supplies of warm clothing, which Montgomery had taken in Montreal, were welcomed by Arnold's troops, who had experienced much suffering in their long, cold marches. The garrison at Quebec defied the Americans, who, through almost daily snow storms, besieged the town for three weeks. Finally, on December 31, 1775, an assault of the fortress was attempted, in which the good and brave Gen. Richard Montgomery fell, and "with him the soul of the expedition fled." The American army went into camp near Quebec, and passed a rigorous winter. Reinforcements from England in the spring of 1776 obliged the patriots to abandon their purpose, and by the middle of June they gave up all foothold on Canada.

84. When were warships first proposed?

Ans. On October 5, 1775, by the Continental Congress, and Washington was authorized to employ two armed vessels to intercept British storeships bound for Quebec.

85. When was the first gun fired in Virginia against the British ?

Ans. On October 26, 1775, at Hampton, to prevent the burning of the town by a British war-vessel under Dunmore.

86. What was the result ?

Ans. Dunmore was driven off and his fleet shattered.

87. What was the last important battle on Colonial ground in 1775 ?

Ans. The battle of Great Bridge, Virginia, twelve miles from Norfolk. After Dunmore's defeat at Hampton, he declared open war. The Virginia militia flew to arms, and prepared breastworks to repulse the British. On December 9th, an attempt by Dunmore to cross the bridge was met by the Virginia sharpshooters. After a struggle of fifteen minutes, the British retreated, losing more than sixty men in killed and wounded. The Virginians lost only one man.

88. How did the year 1776 open in Virginia ?

Ans. Dunmore, who had been royal governor since 1770, infuriated by his want of success at

99734

Hampton and Great Bridge, set fire to the town of Norfolk and destroyed it on January 1, 1776.

89. What was the American situation at Boston in the winter of 1775–'76?

Ans. Washington had strengthened the investment of the city, closely watched the movements of the British, looked after the welfare of his troops, and prepared for action.

90. What was the first effective military movement in that vicinity in 1776?

Ans. On the night of March 4th intrenchments were raised on Dorchester Heights, which menaced the British in Boston and brought consternation to the leaders.

91. What was the result of this movement?

Ans. The British, finding that they would not be able to dislodge the patriots from their vantage ground, decided to evacuate Boston.

92. What is the date of the evacuation of Boston?

Ans. March 17, 1776.

93. How did Washington communicate the news to Congress?

Ans. By a letter dated March 17th, which said: "This morning the ministerial troops evacuated the town of Boston without destroying it, and we are now in full possession."

94. What gave evidence of haste in the flight of the British?

Ans. The stores of military goods which they left. There were 250 cannon, 2,500 chaldrons of seacoal, 25,000 bushels of wheat, 3,000 bushels of barley, 150 horses, bedding and clothing for soldiers, etc.

95. What was Washington's next step?

Ans. He put Boston in a state of security, and supposing that Howe's destination would be New York, he put the main body of his army in motion for that city, and reached there himself on April 14, 1776.

96. What impressions were the foregoing events making on the minds of the Colonists?

Ans. In the opinion of the whole people the necessity of a " Declaration of Independence " was steadily gaining ground.

97. What was the attitude of the Continental Congress toward independence?

Ans. It had begun to realize that a separation must come, and had already authorized measures for defence ; but not till June 7, 1776, did Richard Henry Lee introduce a resolution declaring "these United Colonies are, and of right ought to be, free and independent States."

98. How was this resolution received by the Colonies?

Ans. Before this time, five Colonies (Rhode Island, Virginia, North Carolina, South Carolina and Georgia) had declared for independence, and before June closed all the other Colonies united in this decision.

99. When did Congress meet for a full discussion of the subject?

Ans. On July 1, 1776.

100. What were some of the important committees appointed by Congress to aid in carrying out measures to insure independence?

Ans. (i) Thomas Jefferson, John Adams, Benjamin Franklin, Roger Sherman and Robert R. Livingston were chosen, by ballot, to draft a Declaration of Independence.

(ii) One member from each Colony was named to construct a form of Confederation.

(iii) A plan for "Treaties with Foreign Powers" was intrusted to five members, of which Benjamin Franklin was one.

(iv) A "Board of War" was named, with John Adams at the head.

(v) Congress resolved that "all persons abiding within any of the United Colonies and deriving protection from its laws, owe allegiance to the said laws, and are members of such Colony." The guilt of treason was charged upon "all members of any of the United

Colonies who should be adherent to the King of Great Britain, giving him aid and comfort."

101. When was the resolution in favor of independence adopted by Congress?

Ans. On July 2, 1776.

102. What day is called the Nation's Birthday, and why is it so celebrated?

Ans. The Fourth of July, 1776 ; because on that day the instrument known as "The Declaration of Independence," as prepared in its final form by the committee appointed for that purpose, was reported to Congress, was unanimously adopted by the representatives of twelve of the thirteen Colonies, was signed by John Hancock, President of the Congress, and thus formally severed the political connection between the United States of America and Great Britain. New York's delegates, for want of instructions, did not adopt the Declaration of Independence until July 9th. Between July 4th and August 2d the names of the "Signers" were affixed to the engrossed copy of the historic document.

103. What was the immediate result of this Declaration?

(i) It changed the old thirteen Colonies into free and independent States.

(ii) The war was no longer a civil war. Great Britain was a foreign country.

(iii) Every former subject of the King of England, in the thirteen Colonies, now owed allegiance to the new Republic.

(iv) The States, that were henceforth independent of Great Britain, were not independent of one another.

(v) The United States of America were now one people, assuming powers over war, peace, foreign alliances and commerce.

104. How did the Colonies signify their acquiescence?

Ans. In MASSACHUSETTS the "immortal State paper" was read from the pulpit by each minister to his congregation and entered in the town records.

MARYLAND conjured every virtuous citizen to join cordially in maintaining the freedom of her State and that of the others.

In PHILADELPHIA the "Committee of Safety" and that of "Inspection" marched in procession to the State House, where the Declaration was read to battalions of volunteers and a concourse of inhabitants from the city and county, after which chimes from the churches and peals from the State House bell, proclaimed "Liberty throughout the land."

In NEW JERSEY the Congress of that State in presence of the Committee of Safety, the Militia under arms, and a great assembly of the people published at Trenton the Declaration of Independence and their own Constitution.

In NEW YORK, by command of Washington, the Declaration was read to every brigade in the city, followed by the most hearty approbation. In the evening the equestrian statue of George III. that stood in Bowling Green was pulled down, and the lead eventually run into bullets.

In all the other Colonies (now States) the Declaration was received with similar demonstrations and accepted with unspeakable pleasure.

105. What was the first battle after separation was decided upon?

Ans. The Battle of Sullivan's Island, in South Carolina.

106. Can you give an account of this battle, and its result?

Ans. A large fleet was sent from England in the spring of 1776 to operate on the sea coast of the southern Colonies. They arrived off Charleston bar on the 4th of June. Apprised of their designs, and encouraged by a signal success at Moore's Creek, North Carolina, on the preceding February 27th, the southern patriots responded cheerfully to the call of Gen. John Rutledge, President of the Colony. Several thousand men were gathered in or near Charleston when the enemy appeared.   Six mounted cannon had been erected at Fort Sullivan, commanding the channel, and the fort was garrisoned by about 500 men under Col. William Moultrie.   The British commenced a combined attack on June 28th under Sir Henry Clinton by land, and Sir Peter Parker by sea.   The conflict raged for ten hours, or till nightfall, when the British fleet, almost shattered into fragments, abandoned the enterprise.   Gen. Charles Lee, who had charge of the American land forces, had advised Moultrie to abandon the fort when the British approached, but the brave officer would not desert it, and his victory was so complete that the ladies of Charleston presented him with an elegant stand of colors, and the fort was named "Fort Moultrie."

107. What memorable act of bravery occurred during the fight?

Ans. On one bastion of the fort was displayed the Union flag (the equivalent of our present Federal colors), and on the opposite bastion was hoisted the flag of South Carolina—blue with a white crescent, on which was emblazoned "Liberty."   Early in the action the staff of the latter was shot away, and the colors fell on the beach, outside of the works.   William Jasper, a Sergeant, discovering the loss, leaped through an embrazure, braving the thickest of the fire, took up the flag, returned with it safely, and fastening it to a sponge-staff (used for cleaning cannon), he planted it on the summit next the enemy.

108. What were the dying words of the patriot officer, Macdaniel, during the conflict?

Ans. "I am dying; but don't let the cause of liberty expire with me!"

109. When Washington reached New York from Boston, what were his first measures of defence?

Ans. He proceeded at once to fortify the town and the Hudson Highlands. His force was only about 7,000 men.

110. Where was the British General Howe at this time?

Ans. At Halifax, where he went when driven from Boston.

111. When did he leave Halifax?

Ans. On June 11, 1776, when he sailed for New York, reaching Sandy Hook on the 29th.

112. Where did he land?

Ans. On Staten Island, on July 2d.

113. What accessions did he receive at this point?

Ans. He was here joined by Sir Henry Clinton, who had come up from the South after his defeat at Fort Moultrie, and by his brother, Admiral Howe, with a fleet and large land force from England.

114. How large a British force was thus gathering?

Ans. Including vessels, which were now arriving with hired Hessian troops, 30,000 soldiers, many of them veterans, were ready to meet the American army, on August 1, 1776.

115. What was Washington's force?

Ans. About 17,000 men were intrenched in and around New York, but many of them were unfit for duty.

116. What other adverse influence, besides disparity of troops, had Washington to contend with?

Ans. When General Howe arrived at Staten Island, the inhabitants received him with open arms. The Tories flocked to his standard, organized themselves into companies and battalions, or scattered themselves over the country, and served as spies, to give information, or, as opportunity afforded, harass the people.

117. What was Howe's first move?

Ans. To land on Long Island, which he did without opposition.

118. What was the date of his landing on Long Island?

Ans. August 22, 1776, and during the day 10,000 effective British soldiers were landed between Fort Hamilton and Gravesend Village.

119. How had Washington prepared for this encroachment of the British?

Ans. He had disposed his main army on Manhattan Island, as a guard to the city of New York, but had sent out detachments to the most exposed points in the vicinity. The largest detachment was sent to Brooklyn, under General Sullivan, who occupied a fortified camp opposite New York. Generals Putnam and Stirling were also in command of forces on the island.

120. By whom were the British forces on the island led?

Ans. By Sir Henry Clinton, Gen. James Grant, Lord Percy, Lord Cornwallis, and the Hessian commander, De Heister.

121. When did the fighting begin?

Ans. Before dawn on the morning of August 27, 1776.

122. What was the result?

Ans. The Americans were defeated at all points. They were opposed by veterans and a much superior force, and it was like leading a forlorn hope. At noon the victory for the British was complete.

123. What loss was sustained by the British?

Ans About five hunderd in killed, wounded and prisoners.

124 What was the loss of the Americans?

Ans. Five hundred killed and wounded and eleven hundred made prisoners. Many of the captives were consigned to the Sugar House on Liberty street and the prison ships in Wallabout Bay. The hard lot of these prisoners made the fate of those who perished in battle an enviable one.

125. What occurred on the night of August 29?

Ans. While Howe and his troops were resting, secure of their prey as they thought, under cover of a heavy fog Washington silently withdrew his shattered army, and as the sunlight fell upon the river, the last boat-load of patriots had reached New York. While the Long Island defeat was a distressing one, and on many accounts the most so of any during the war, Washington's masterful retreat was one of the greatest achievements of the seven years' struggle. Aided by the sea-fog, which came rolling in from the ocean, shrouding the British camp, hanging over the East River and hiding Brooklyn (without enveloping New York). Washington remained standing on the ferry stair and would not enter his boat till all were embarked.

126. What was the date of this landing in New York?

Ans. August 30, 1776.   At seven o'clock in the morning Washington stepped on shore, having before him nearly 9,000 men with their provisions, military stores, field artillery and ordnance.

127. What was the effect of this retreat upon Howe?

Ans. He was greatly chagrined, and prepared to make an attack on New York before the Americans should be reinforced or escape.

128. What was Washington's next move?

Ans. Seeing a disposition on the part of Howe to hem him in by sending land forces, by way of the East river to the upper part of the Island, and also feeling sure that the English fleet in New York harbor would render his position untenable, he decided on the 12th of September to remove military stores to a secure place, at Dobbs Ferry, on the Hudson, and retreat to and fortify Harlem Heights.

129. When did the British take possession of New York?

Ans. On September 15, 1776.

130. When was the next encounter between the two forces?

Ans. On September 16th, at Harlem Heights.

This was a severe skirmish in which the Americans were victorious; but it cost the lives of two brave American officers, Colonel Knowlton of Connecticut, and Major Leitch of Virginia.

131. What was Howe's next manœuvre?

Ans. Leaving a strong force in possession of New York on September 20th, he sent three armed vessels up the Hudson to cut off the Americans from communication with the western shore, and fresh troops from England made their way to a point in Westchester County, beyond the Harlem.

132. What was Howe's apparent purpose?

Ans. To form a connection with the large body of troops in Canada, who would secure the Hudson and its Highlands, and with his command around New York, prevent the Americans' escape through New Jersey, and oblige them to surrender.

133. What means did Washington employ to gain an exact knowledge of the plans of the British at this time?

Ans. He called for a volunteer to enter the British camp, and accepted the services of young Capt. Nathan Hale. Captain Hale belonged to Colonel Knowlton's Connecticut troops. He was only 21 years of age, a graduate of Yale College and an ardent patriot.

134. What was the result of Hale's attempt?

Ans. On September 22nd, while in the above service, he was caught within the British lines, avowed his name and his purpose, and was executed in what is now New York City, as a spy.   His last words were: "I only regret that I have but one life to lose for my country."   A monument has been erected to his memory in City Hall Park, New York.

135. What battles occurred in October, 1776, in the North?

Ans. On the 11th and 13th the British, under Carleton, met Colonel Arnold, with his command, who had been stationed at Fort Ticonderoga and Crown Point during the summer. A naval encounter on Lake Champlain ensued, and the Americans were obliged to burn their fleet and retire.   Carleton, however, though at the gateway to the Hudson, did not follow up his success by taking Ticonderoga, but returned to winter quarters in Canada, reserving that conquest for a glorious opening of his next campaign, and awaiting tidings from Howe.

136. How did Washington meet the strategy of the enemy?

Ans. Perceiving their designs to shut him in, he placed a garrison of nearly 3,000 men at Fort Washington and withdrew the remainder of his army to White Plains. There, on October 28, 1776, there was a severe engagement. The Americans were driven from their position, but formed a strong camp at North Castle, about five miles above.

137. What was the effect of the battle of White Plains on the British?

Ans. Howe decided not to risk an attack upon Washington in his present stronghold, and on November 4th he returned to New York by way of Dobbs Ferry.

138. What investigations of the Hudson and its approaches near the Highlands did Washington now make?

Ans. On November 11th and 12th he went with Generals Heath, Stirling, Mifflin, and James and George Clinton to make an examination of this vicinity.

139. What were his instructions in regard to the Highlands?

Ans. He gave Heath the command of the posts on both sides of the river, with 3,000 men from Massachusetts, Connecticut and New York to secure them.

140. Where did Washington then go?

Ans. Having already sent about five thousand men into New Jersey under General Putnam, he crossed the river, and took up his position at Hackensack, six miles from Fort Lee, on November 14, 1776.

141. What was the fate of Fort Washington?

Ans. On November 16th, it was taken by the Hessians under Rahl and Knyphausen. The American's loss in killed and wounded was not very large ; but besides the loss of much valuable artillery and military stores, 2,600 were taken prisoners, many of them well-trained soldiers, and, like the captives taken on Long Island, they were consigned to the prison ships.

142. What was the next loss by the Americans?

Ans. On the approach of a large force of English and Hessians, Fort Lee, on the Jersey shore, opposite Fort Washington, was evacuated November 20, 1776.

143. What were some of the facts of interest in this evacuation?

Ans. Washington, still in Hackensack, received word that the British had crossed the Hudson at Closter Landing, and that Cornwallis was on his way to Fort Lee. Mounting his charger, in three-quarters of an hour Washington reached the fort, took the command of the troops stationed there, and led them down the hill, and through the valley of the Hackensack river, and over "New Bridge" in safety.

Less than three hours afterward, a detachment from Cornwallis's command came up to the river, but the Americans had burned the bridge behind them, and the English forces retired.

144. What was the danger to the army in Hackensack ?

Ans. The possibility of being hemmed in between the Passaic and Hackensack rivers.

145. How did Washington prevent this ?

Ans. He moved his army to Newark, beyond the Passaic, on November 21st.

146. What difficulty did Washington encounter in his command ?

Ans. The insubordination of Gen. Charles Lee, who, with one-half of Washington's force under him, was never ready to obey the command of his superior.

147. What threatened Washington in the rear ?

Ans. Cornwallis was still advancing, and reached Newark on November 28th, as the Americans left the town.

148. Where did Washington go from Newark ?

Ans. Directly to New Brunswick ; but after a short rest he moved on across the Raritan, breaking down the bridge as he retreated. Cornwallis again was just too late, though a sharp cannonading took place across the river.

149. Where did the army rest on December 2, 1776?

Ans. At Princeton, where Washington left Stirling with 1,200 men, and then moved down to Trenton. From there, transferring his baggage and stores across the Delaware, he faced about, with such troops as were fit for duty, to resist the progress of the enemy.

150. On his way to Princeton, what occurred?

Ans. He met Stirling retreating before a large force, and he also returned and crossed the Delaware on December 8th.

151. What did the British do when the Americans retreated?

Ans. They remained at Princeton for several hours, and then taking up the march for Trenton they arrived just in time to see the last boat of the patriots safely pass the river.

152. Why did not the British immediately follow?

Ans. For lack of transportation. Washington had secured or destroyed every boat on the river for miles.

153. Where did the British main force lie?

Ans. On the east side of the Delaware, where 'Howe held a strong reserve at New.Brunswick, with detachments at Pennington, Trenton, Princeton, Bordentown and Burlington.

154. For what is December 13, 1776, memorable?

Ans. The capture of Gen. Charles Lee, who, though second in command, had continually acted in direct opposition to Washington, criticising all the movements of the Commander-in-Chief.   He was taken in New Jersey by a scouting party of the British, and sent to New York as prisoner.   He was exchanged in 1777, but acted the traitor till his death in Philadelphia in 1782.

155. What reinforcement now came to Washington?

Ans. Retaining his position on the west bank of the Delaware, he was strengthened by Lee's command, now under Sullivan, and three regiments from Ticonderoga under General Stark.

156. What was now Washington's plan?

Ans. To re-cross the Delaware and attack the enemy in their separate detachments.

157. What time was set for this movement, and against whom was it to be first directed?

Ans. The night of December 25, 1776.   The Hessians, now at Trenton under Rahl (who had been prominent in the affairs at White Plains and Fort Washington), were to be the first object of attack.

158. What were the main features of this movement?

Ans. At dusk, on Christmas night, 1776, the troops selected for this purpose (2,400 men and twenty pieces of artillery), began to cross the Delaware, at " McKonkey's Ferry," nine miles above Trenton.   Imagination can hardly depict the scene.   The cold was intense.   A storm of snow and hail was raging, and floating ice rendered the river well-nigh impassable.   Though the Delaware at this point was only 600 feet wide, its passage by heavily laden flat-boats was difficult in the extreme, and it was four o'clock on the morning of the 26th, when the troops were mustered on the Jersey shore.   Fortunately the storm kept every one within doors, concealing the approach of troops, with artillery, over the frozen grounds.   The Hessians, (as Washington foresaw), had spent Christmas day and night in sports and festivities, and Rahl was indulging in wine and cards up to the moment of the attack.   The surprise was complete.   Between forty and fifty Hessians were killed, and more than one thousand prisoners were taken.   Rahl, who received his death-blow, was held up by his men for the act of surrender.   Of the Americans, two were frozen to death and two killed.   The military stores taken were also large.

159. What was the effect of this victory on the English ?

Ans. The contempt of the British forces for the "rebels" was changed to respect and fear. Cornwallis, who was about to embark for England, was ordered by Howe to return to New Jersey and prepare for a winter's campaign.

160. How did the year 1777 open in the American army?

Ans. Washington's achievement had given life and spirit to the whole body of troops.   He crossed the Delaware into Pennsylvania again, immediately after the success of December 26th, taking with him more than one thousand prisoners; but he was not yet ready to give up New Jersey to the British and their minions.   Therefore he recrossed the river again and took up post at Trenton, on the 1st and 2d of January, 1777; and here with an army of less than five thousand he awaited Cornwallis, who came on the 2d with the flower of the British army to encounter him.

161. What was the result of this encounter?

Ans. Washington was obliged to retreat from the town, but the enemy were harassed by musketry from houses and barns, and night coming on they decided to put off the fight till morning.

162. While the British reposed, what was done in the camp of the Americans?

Ans. Leaving his camp fires burning, and a

working party busily and noisily at work till daybreak, Washington swept around the British by country roads, fell upon the troops near Princeton, routed them, took over 200 prisoners, and by rapid marches reached Morristown Heights on January 4, 1777.

163. How was Cornwallis apprised of this defeat?

Ans. By the report of a cannon in the direction of Princeton, on the morning of January 3d. Having waited at Trenton for morning, to make the attack on the Americans, he then discovered that Washington had outgeneraled him.

164. What was the effect of these battles at Trenton and Princeton on the States?

Ans. These surprising successes were hailed with thrilling emotions by a disheartened Nation, and with these victories originated the expression, "Great news from the Jerseys."

165. What was accomplished during the remaining months of the winter of 1776-'77?

Ans. Washington remained in Morristown, and establishing cantonments at different points from Princeton to the Hudson Highlands, he sent out detachments to harass the perplexed British. These expeditions were conducted with so much skill and spirit that on the 1st of

March, 1777, not a British or Hessian soldier could be found in New Jersey except at New Brunswick and Amboy.

166. Where was Howe during this time?

Ans. In New York City, asking for reinforcements, with which he would "finish the war in a year."

167. What occurred in Connecticut on April 25, 1777?

Ans. Tryon, at the head of 2,000 Hessians and British, went up Long Island Sound to Connecticut, marched to Danbury, pillaged and burned the town, and cruelly treated the inhabitants. Ridgefield was also raided at this time.

168. What did a band of Connecticut patriots accomplish on May 22, 1777?

Ans. Colonel Meigs crossed the Sound from Guilford with 170 men, and on the 23d attacked a British provision post at Sag Harbor, burned the storehouse and contents and a dozen vessels, and secured ninety prisoners, without losing a man.

169. What action did Howe take in June?

Ans. He passed over from New York to New Brunswick with his main body of troops, and essayed to draw Washington (who was now strongly posted at Middlebrook) into an engagement. Not succeeding, he suddenly retreated on June 19th, sending some troops to Staten Island. Then suddenly changing front, he attempted to gain Washington's rear; but after Stirling's brigade had maintained a severe skirmish with Cornwallis, the Americans regained their camp, and five days afterward, on June 30th, the whole British army crossed over to Staten Island, leaving New Jersey in complete possession of the patriots.

170. How was the 4th of July, 1777, celebrated in Philadelphia?

Ans. This first anniversary of the "Declaration of Independence" was hailed with a feeling of security and triumph. Bells rang all the day and evening. Ships floated the new flag of the nation, and fireworks, bonfires and a general illumination showed the joy of the people.

171. What was the next movement in the North?

Ans. On July 5, 1777, Burgoyne compelled the Americans to evacuate Fort Ticonderoga, and two days later a detachment of his army defeated them in a severe battle at Hubbardtown. Fort Anne and Fort Edward were also abandoned—the latter on July 22d.

172. What was the object of this movement of the British in the North?

Ans. To form a union with the British forces around New York by way of the Hudson.

173. At the same time, what diverting move did Howe make toward the South?

Ans. Leaving Gen. Henry Clinton in command in New York, he embarked with a fleet of 18,000 troops for the South early in July, 1777.

174. How did this affect Washington's movements?

Ans. Leaving a strong force on the Hudson, Washington went with his main body to Philadelphia.

175. What French ally met him there?

Ans. General Lafayette, a wealthy French nobleman, who having heard of the American struggle and read the Declaration of Independence, was fired with inspirations to give aid to the patriots. Lafayette had already offered his services to the Continental Congress, and he received the commission of Major-General on July 31, 1777. He was introduced to Washington at a public dinner, on August 3d, and in less than forty days was gallantly fighting for freedom in America.

176. What important battles occurred early in August, 1777?

Ans. A British force under Colonel Barry and Lieutenant Leger ascended the St. Lawrence and landing at Oswego laid seige to Fort Stanwix (now Fort Schuyler) on August 3d. On the 6th, a force of 800 militia led by General Herkimer, when marching to relieve Fort Stanwix, fell into an ambush near Oriskany, where one of the fiercest battles of the whole Revolutionary War was fought. Both sides claimed a victory. Herkimer, mortally wounded, drove the enemy away, but was obliged to retreat.

177. What was the result at Fort Stanwix ?

Ans. Overtures from the British commandant were made with much threatening language to which Colonel Willett replied in words of such spirit and bravery, as left no doubt in the minds of the enemy, and on August 22d, when reinforcements were ready to do battle at the Fort, the British suddenly broke camp and fled in such haste and confusion as to leave their tents, a great part of their artillery, camp equipage and baggage.

178. While the seige of Fort Stanwix was in progress, what was done by Burgoyne ?

Ans. While in possession of Fort Edward, he learned that stores of provisions and military supplies had been collected by the patriots at Bennington, and hoping to secure them for his own command, he sent an expedition with verbal orders to march directly to Bennington, take these supplies and then march at once to Albany. In compliance with this order a force of about two thousand moved on towards Bennington; but before reaching there, they were entrapped by Col. John Stark, when 700 prisoners were taken, and more than 200 left dead on the field, with the loss of many officers. A large number of cannon were taken as trophies of victory. This "battle of Bennington" occurred on August 16, 1777. The Americans' loss was 14 killed and 42 wounded.

179. What was a sequel to this brilliant victory?

Ans. It enabled the Americans to send a force in Burgoyne's rear, and cut him off from Lake Champlain.

180. What encounter occurred in Virginia on September 1, 1777?

Ans. The Battle of Fort Henry, where Wheeling, W. Va., now stands. This fort was named for Patrick Henry, then Governor of Virginia. Great Britain had left no stone unturned to secure the favor of the Indians, and on September 1st this fort was assailed by 350 of the Wyandotte and other tribes, who had been supplied with provisions, arms and ammunition by Hamilton, the British Governor at

Detroit.. Supposing the Indians to be few in number, a detachment of fourteen men was sent out to meet the invaders, but they were driven in with almost an entire loss. Afterwards, preceded by a drum and fife and a British flag, the enemy approached, displaying the scalps which had just been torn from their hapless victims. On the morning of the 2d help from other forts arrived, and at last what seemed a defeat was turned into victory. The feats of daring in that encounter were among the most remarkable in the history of the Revolution.

181. What was Howe's destination on leaving New York in July, 1777?

Ans. After waiting in New York Harbor, with his 300 sail, till near August, he moved to the South, and entering the Chesapeake he disembarked at the head of the Bay on August 25th.

182. How did Washington respond to this move of Howe?

Ans. Surmising that Howe intended to go to Philadelphia, he crossed the Delaware, and marched to oppose him. With 11,000 men he met him at Brandywine Creek, with double that force, on September 11th. In the encounter, Washington was obliged to retire from the

field, but in various skirmishes he detained
Howe two weeks on his march of twenty-six
miles to Philadelphia. The British entered
that city on September 26th, making their encampment at Germantown, four miles away.

183. What was being done in September,
1777, near Albany ?

Ans. On the 13th Burgoyne crossed the Hudson, and without the aid from Sir Henry Clinton, which he had expected, he was engaged
from September 19th to October 7th at Bemis
Heights, Stillwater, and Saratoga, in encounters with the patriots, ending in his surrender
on October 17th.   Burgoyne's surrender is
ranked by military critics as the turning point
of the Revolution, and Sir Edward Creasy
ranks Saratoga as one of the fifteen decisive
battles of the world.

184. What battle occurred on October 4,
1777, in Pennsylvania, and what was the result ?

Ans. The battle of Germantown.   The
Americans had nearly become victorious, when,
a fog arising, one American battalion fired into
another, causing a sudden panic, and hence a
defeat.

185. What was accomplished in October,
1777, by the British on the Hudson ?

Ans. Sir Henry Clinton, who had superseded Howe in command at New York, went with a strong force to the Highlands, and on October 13th captured Forts Clinton and Montgomery. Marauding parties went above this point, in hope of drawing off some of the patriot forces around Saratoga. They burned Kingston, but, hearing of the surrender of Burgoyne, they hastily retreated, and Clinton and his army returned to New York.

186. What was threatening the British in Philadelphia ?

Ans. Fort Mifflin in Pennsylvania and Fort Mercer in New Jersey, both on the Delaware, near Philadelphia, shut the army off from supplies, and there was danger of starvation. After severe and prolonged assaults, the forts were taken on November 19, 1777.

187. What attempt to vanquish the Americans did Howe make before going into winter quarters at Philadelphia?

Ans. He announced to his government that he should make a forward movement on the "rebels," and on the night of December 4, 1777, he marched out with 14,000 men to attack the American lines. Washington, whose keenness of sight had been developed by his early forest life, had selected strong ground for encampment in the woods of White Marsh, fourteen miles from Philadelphia. At night the British force rested on their arms about three miles from the Americans, and the fires of the two armies illuminated the country for miles around. Though Washington had but 7,000 effective men he desired an engagement, but Howe instead marched back on the 5th to Germantown. Returning on the 6th, as if intending a surprise, he reconnoitered all day. Nothing occurred, however, except a sharp action on Edge Hill, when the British lost eighty-nine, and the Americans lost the brave Major Morris of New Jersey and twenty-seven soldiers. Howe returned to Philadelphia, and passed the winter behind his entrenchments, and thus, on December 8th, the campaign closed, Washington having no choice but to seek winter quarters for his suffering army.

188. Where were these winter quarters found?

Ans. At Valley Forge on the Schuylkill, twenty-one miles from Philadelphia.

189. What was there to recommend this location for an encampment?

Ans. The ground lay between two ridges of hills, and was covered with forest trees. Washington saw in these trees a town of log cabins affording shelter, to save the army from dis-

persion, and on December 19th it was encamped
at Valley Forge, within a day's march of
Howe's forces, but with no covering till they
could build their own houses.   Without tents,
blankeis, clothing or shoes, the work of the
Christmas holidays changed the forest into huts,
thatched with boughs, in the order of a regular
encampment.   Washington's vigilance securing
against surprise, love of country, and attach-
ment to their commander, sustained the patriots
during their distressing hardships.

190. What assistance did Washington receive
in preparing his troops for future action ?

Ans. Baron Steuben, a Prussian officer, had
adopted America for his country, and on February 23, 1778, he was welcomed at Valley
Forge, where he wrought a reform in the use
of the musket and in manœuvring of troops.

191. What assistance came from France ?

Ans. Through the efforts of Benjamin Franklin a French alliance was formed, and a treaty
was signed on February 6, 1778, by which the
Americans bound themselves to accept no terms
of peace till Great Britain should recognize the
independence of the United States.

192. When did news of the French alliance
reach Washington's army ?

Ans. On May 6, 1778, and the patriots at

Valley Forge celebrated the event with fitting ceremonies.

193. How had the British in Philadelphia passed the winter?

Ans. The soldiers had been well provided for, the officers being quartered on the inhabitants. The days were spent in pastime and the nights in entertainments.

194. What were some of the means used to obtain supplies for the British?

Ans. Detachments were sent out into New Jersey and the country round, and by inhuman assaults on forts and villages they returned to Germantown laden with spoils.

195. What was the first movement of the French government in compliance with its treaty with the United States?

Ans. A squadron was dispatched to blockade the British fleet in the Delaware.

196. What was the effect of the French movement upon the British?

Ans. Sir Henry Clinton, now in command, withdrew his whole army from Philadelphia on June 18, 1778.

197. How was Clinton's plan in a measure frustrated?

Ans. He intended to go to New York by way of Amboy. He had with him 11,000 men, and a large baggage and provision train. Washington immediately broke camp at Valley Forge, and pursued Clinton with more than an equal force. Clinton was compelled to change his course, in the direction of Sandy Hook, and he was harassed in flank and rear by the New Jersey militia.

198. What celebrated battle occurred at this time ?

Ans. The Battle of Monmouth, on June 26, 1778.

199. What was the result ?

Ans. A terrible contest raged all day, and when night came, both armies were glad of a cessation of hostilities. The Americans rested on their arms, intending to renew the fight at dawn; but when dawn came the British camp was found to be deserted.

200. Where did Clinton go ?

Ans. His shattered forces boarded the British fleet lying at Sandy Hook, and he went with them to New York, which was British headquarters until the war ended.

201. Where did Washington then go ?

Ans. To New Brunswick, N. J., and thence across the Hudson to White Plains, which he reached on July 20, 1778, and where he remained till late autumn.

202. With what terrible massacre did July, 1778, open ?

Ans. A party of British rangers and Indians, under Col. John Butler (a most brutal Tory), went down the Tioga river, and in the Wyoming valley murdered with ruthless cruelty men, women and children. The strong men who might have protected this region, were on duty in distant parts, and the destruction of homes was complete. The British leader boasted that he had burned a thousand houses and every mill. This is called the "Massacre of Wyoming."

203. What other encounter occurred with the British, who had still the Indians and Tories for allies?

Ans. George Rogers Clark, a young Virginian, learning that Hamilton, the British commandant at Detroit, had made a plan to induce all the Western tribes to make war upon the frontier, undertook to carry the war into the enemy's country. By a masterly movement, begun in July, 1778, he defeated and captured Hamilton, and ended (in February, 1779) by holding the whole country north of the Ohio, from the Alleghanies to the Mississippi.

204. What was the situation in Rhode Island in July and August, 1778?

Ans. On July 29th the French fleet, arriving off Newport, forced the English to destroy ten of their war vessels. On August 10th a British fleet of thirty-four sail appearing before Newport, the French fleet gave chase, but the English got away without a fight.

205. What other engagements occurred in August, 1778, in Rhode Island?

Ans. The land forces of the patriots were defeated at Quaker Hill and Newport Island.

206. What notable massacre by the British with assistance from the Tories took place September 27, 1778?

Ans. A force of patriots was quartered in the village of New Tappan, Rockland County, N. Y., and another command was at Old Tappan or Harrington near the Hackensack river. Cornwallis, on a foraging expedition on the west bank of the Hudson, finding these troops comparatively defenseless, came upon them at evening and every one of the force was bayoneted without quarter.

207. What were some of the outrages committed in October, 1778?

Ans. The British, still depending on the Tory allies, spread themselves over New Jersey, destroying the shipping at Little Egg Harbor, burning towns and villages and laying waste the surrounding lands. On the night of October 15th, they surprised the infantry under command of Pulaski (the Polish nobleman, who had been made Brigadier General) but, instead of cumbering themselves with prisoners, killed all they could.

208. When did the Cherry Valley massacre occur?

Ans. On November 11, 1778. The fort was found to be too strong to take, but the band of Indians, Tories and regulars raided the town, murdered and scalped the inhabitants, many of them women and children. The story of these massacres, repeated from village to village, only strengthened the purpose of resistance.

209. What had been accomplished by the two armies during the fall months of 1778?

Ans. Washington's force at White Plains had been comparatively quiet, owing to the inactivity of the British, who still had their headquarters on Manhattan Island.

210. What move did Washington make in December, 1778?

Ans. Convinced that the enemy had no present designs for operating in New England, he prepared to put his army into favorable winter quarters. Six brigades were cantoned on the east of the Hudson and at West Point. One brigade was placed in the rear of Haverstraw, one at Elizabethtown, and seven at Middlebrook, where he made his headquarters, as in the previous year.

211. What plan of the British was developed at the close of the year 1778?

Ans. To carry the war into the Southern States. Sir Henry Clinton sent about 2,000 troops under Colonel Campbell to invade Georgia, as being the weakest member of the confederacy, and on December 29, 1778, they captured Savannah. They retained the city as headquarters until 1782.

212. How did the year 1779 open?

Ans. Though the British had made no headway in conquering the Colonies, the year opened gloomily for the patriots, for lack of money with which to prosecute the war.

213. What plan did Congress make for the campaign of 1779?

Ans. It resolved to act on the defensive, except in retaliatory measures against the Indians and Tories in the interior and on the frontier.

214. How were the British carrying out their plan for separating the Southern Colonies from the Northern?

Ans. They had captured Savannah on December 29, 1778, and early in January, 1779, Brigadier-General Prevost (who had been successful in subduing Florida) marched as a con-

queror across lower Georgia, capturing Fort
Sunbury, on the 9th, on his way to Savannah.
Colonel Campbell, who had been sent from
New York to co-operate with Prevost, with 800
Hessians, took possession of Augusta.

215. Who was then commanding the southern army of patriots?

Ans. Gen. Benjamin Lincoln, of Massachusetts.

216. Where was he located at the opening of
the 1779 campaign?

Ans. On the South Carolina side of the Savannah river.

217. What was the first success by the patriots
in this campaign?

Ans. On February 3, 1779, the enemy were
defeated at Beaufort, S. C.

218. What was the next American success?

Ans. On February 14th Col. Andrew Pickens defeated Colonel Boyd, and his large acces-
sion of Tories, at Kettle Creek, Ga.

219. What was an important effect of this
success?

Ans. The Tories of the Carolinas never again
assembled except in small parties.

220. When did the last engagement in the
spring of 1779 occur in Georgia.

Ans. On March 3d, at Briar Creek, where, in

consequence of lack of precaution on the part of General Ashe, the patriots were defeated, After this success, General Prevost proclaimed a sort of civil government in Georgia.

221. How was Sir Henry Clinton employing his forces in the North?

Ans. He was sending out marauding expeditions, to plunder and harass the people on the seacoast. On March 25th and 26th, they dispersed the Americans at Greenwich, Conn., and General Putnam barely escaped capture by some dragoons. He afterwards rallied his troops and recaptured much of the plunder and took thirty-eight prisoners.

222. What measures did Congress institute in retaliation for the massacres of the summer of 1778?

Ans. It directed Washington to protect the inland frontier, and chastise the Indians who had been engaged in these massacres.

223 What was the first movement against the Indians in pursuance of these instructions?

Ans. Before a great expedition was ready, Colonel Van Schaick and Colonel Willett made a swift move upon the Onondagas, on April 20, 1779, and destroyed their settlement without the loss of a man.

224. What engagement occurred in the South on May 11, 1779 ?

Ans. General Prevost attempted to take Charleston, and approaching Charleston Neck demanded a surrender, which was promptly refused. A letter having been intercepted from General Lincoln (commander of the patriots in the South), which charged General Moultrie not to give up the city, as he was hastening to his relief, caused the British to retreat in the night.

225. What other operations took place in the South in May ?

Ans. The British entered Hampton Roads, Va., and, co-operating with land forces, spread desolation on both sides of the Elizabeth River from the Roads to Norfolk and Portsmouth. After destroying a vast amount of property, they withdrew, and at the close of the month of May were assisting Sir Henry Clinton on the Hudson.

226. What engagement occurred in South Carolina in June, 1779?

Ans. On the 20th at Stono Ferry, the patriots drove the enemy with great precipitation into their works. The hot season now coming on, hostilities in the South were suspended.

227. What successful manœuvre did Sir Henry Clinton execute on June 1st ?

Ans. He moved on the Hudson Highlands and took Stony Point and Verplanck's Point. These points were the termini of King's Ferry, which had been the crossing place for Washington between Connecticut and New Jersey.

228. Why did Clinton not continue his march to the North?

Ans. The rapid movement of General Washington and his forces prevented his going farther. Therefore, leaving strong garrisons at each of the above posts, he returned to New York.

229. How did July, 1779, open?

Ans. By a skirmish at Bedford and Pound Ridge in Westchester County, N. Y., when Colonel Tarleton was obliged to retire, though he burned dwellings and churches in his retreat.

230. What invasions on the seacoast of Connecticut did the British make in July, 1779?

Ans. Tryon, who had burned Danbury in the previous year, landed at New Haven on July 5th, plundered the town, and laid Fairfield and Norwalk in ashes.

231. What brilliant action occurred on July 16, 1779?

Ans. The recapture of Stony Point by "Mad" Anthony Wayne. It was retaken by a surprise at night, and at two in the morning Wayne, wounded in the head and supported by two aids, wrote to Washington : "The fort and garrison are ours."

232. Where was the next fight ?

Ans. On July 19th Maj. Henry Lee surprised a British garrison at Paulus Hook, (now Jersey City,) and took the fort and 160 prisoners.

233. In carrying out the instructions of Congress in regard to the frontier, what were some of the engagements ?   -

Ans. An ancient settlement in the western part of Orange County, New York, called Minisink, met with unusual severity, by the Indians and Tories. On July 22, 1779, a small band . under Colonel Hathorn, of the Warwick regiment, attempted to rout the enemy, but the latter were too strong for the patriots, who were themselves routed. At Chemung (now Elmira) a body of Indians and Tories, strongly fortified, was dispersed, and in the course of a few weeks forty Indian villages were destroyed. These retaliations continued till the end of September, 1779, but the beneficial effects on the young Republic were questionable.   ·

234. What naval exploit made the year 1779 famous ?   -

Ans. The capture of the British war vessel

"Serapis" by the "Bon Homme Richard," commanded by John Paul Jones, on September 23d. Jones, who was born in Scotland, came to Virginia in boyhood, entered the American naval service in 1775, and in 1779 he was burning shipping in British ports and threatening Edinburgh. His capture of two British war ships off Flamborough Head (the "Serapis" and "Countess of Scarborough"), after one of the most desperate sea fights on record, was one of the most remarkable occurrences in the naval annals of the war.

235. How was the summer campaign of 1779 brought to a close?

Ans. By the defeat of the patriots who had laid siege to Savannah on September 23d. General Lincoln, with the aid of the French fleet under Count D'Estaing, was unsuccessful, and the losses to the Americans were great. Pulaski, the brave Pole, and Samuel Jasper, who so bravely replaced the fallen flag at Fort Moultrie in 1776, were sacrificed.

236. What was accomplished in October, 1779?

Ans. Very little, except the withdrawal of the British troops from Rhode Island, which was done, October 25.

237. What caused the British to evacuate Rhode Island?

Ans. Lafayette, who had been in France during the summer, had induced the French to send another powerful fleet and several thousand troops to aid the Americans. Clinton, having learned of this intended expedition, called to New York all of his troops at the North.

238. What occurred during the two remaining months of 1779?

Ans. Clinton sailed for the South on December 25th with about 5,000 troops to open a vigorous campaign in the Carolinas, and Washington went into winter quarters at Morristown.

239. What was the condition of the army of patriots when the year 1780 came in?

Ans. With headquarters at Morristown, N. J., the army was obliged to remain inactive for lack of means to prosecute the war. The suffering of the soldiers for want of blankets and clothing, and often for lack of food, was nearly as great as in that trying winter at Valley Forge in 1778. The winter of 1779–1780 was also unusually severe. It was remembered as the coldest winter the Colonists had ever known, and snow fell almost continuously from early November, 1779, till March, 1780. New York bay and the Hudson river were as firm as land. People crossed Long Island Sound, from

Connecticut to Lloyd's Neck, a distance of twelve miles, on the ice. The Raritan river in New Jersey was frozen solid for months. The soldiers were employed much of the time in breaking roads for all their supplies, having the co-operation of the inhabitants with their teams. Sallies were occasionally made by both armies, but nothing of moment occurred till spring opened. In the latter part of March, 1780, 400 British Hessians from New York raided the country in New Jersey as far as the northern line, and westward to Hackensack. Their brutality was long remembered.

240. When did Clinton open his campaign in the South?

Ans. On April 10, 1780, Clinton, having passed Fort Moultrie, summoned Charleston to surrender. Escape by evacuation was no longer possible for Lincoln, as he was surrounded by many thousand troops, with Clinton, Arbuthnot and Cornwallis in command, and he therefore capitulated with his whole army on May 12th.

241. After this success, where did Clinton go?

Ans. He returned to New York, leaving Cornwallis in command, and South Carolina was soon overcome by the British.

242. What was the condition of the people in South Carolina at this time?

Ans. That of abject submission. Though there were many at heart Tories, the mass of the people were suffering from terror. Cornwallis was brutal in the extreme. Confiscation and other punishments were inflicted on all patriots, and massacres were common.

243. What was the first important battle after that of Charleston?

Ans. That of Camden, South Carolina. With great exertion, a new American army was collected in North Carolina, with additions from Virginia, and the command was given to Gates. He showed himself wholly incapable, and on August 16, 1780, Cornwallis defeated him at Camden, nearly destroying his army.

244. What was the result of the last two battles?

Ans. All organized resistance to Great Britain ceased in the South.

245. What noted patriot leaders now came to the front?

Ans. Marion, Sumter, Pickens and Henry Lee, and through all discouragements they kept the patriots in heart.

246. What was lending a ray of hope to the Americans at the North?

Ans. De Grasse and Rochambeau, with the French fleet and several thousand soldiers, landed at Newport on July 12, 1780.

247. What infamous act of perfidy by an American General was discovered in September, 1780 ?

Ans. The treason of Benedict Arnold—one of the bravest and most brilliant American Generals in battle, but a man of weak moral character.

248. What was the nature of his treason ?

Ans. Hurt by alleged injustice to him in the matter of promotions and smarting under a repremand for mal-administration in Philadelphia, he concerted with the enemy to betray the strategic line of the Hudson into their possession.

249. How did he obtain the desired opportunity ?

Ans. He asked for and obtained from Washington the command of the fortress at West Point.

250. Before obtaining this command, what preliminary treasonable measures had he taken ?

Ans. He had corresponded with Sir Henry Clinton through Major André for several months.   In this correspondence through André (Clinton's Adjutant-General), he bargained to betray West Point and its dependencies into the hands of the British.   For this service he was to receive a Brigadier's commission and $50,000 in money.

251. How did he proceed with these plans ?

Ans. He chose a time when Washington was absent in Hartford, Conn., conferring with Rochambeau, commander of the French fleet, which had reached Newport on July 10th. André met Arnold by appointment on September 22, 1780, at Haverstraw, on the west side of the Hudson. By their plans then concluded, Clinton was to sail up the river with a strong force, and after a show of resistance Arnold was to surrender West Point.

252. What circumstance defeated their plan ?

Ans. The "Vulture," in which André went up the river, was driven from her anchorage by shots from the shore, fired by Lieut. James Livingston, while André was in consultation with Arnold, and André was obliged to cross the river and make his way by land to New York.

253. What was his experience at Tarrytown ?

Ans. He was stopped and searched by three young Militia-men, who finding papers concealed in his boots, took him to the nearest American post.

254. With what result ?

Ans. The papers thus found revealed the plot. Arnold, the alarmed traitor, escaped and found safety with the British in New York, and André was hanged as a spy, October 2, 1780.

255. How did Congress show its appreciation to the three Militia men who secured André?

Ans. On November 3, 1780, it voted to each a silver medal and a pension of $200 a year for life.

256. What was a sign that the tide was turning in favor of the Americans?

Ans. A decisive victory on October 7, 1780, at King's Mountain, S. C. This was a signal success inasmuch as it was effected by a people who had been regarded as conquered and powerless. It was a popular triumph by troops who, in the most part, went into the fight without the expectation or hope of reward, and it was a beginning of a series of victories.

257. Where was Arnold found in 1781?

Ans. In the service of Sir Henry Clinton, who sent him with 1,600 men to make a series of depredations in lower Virginia. He burned Richmond on January 5th, devastated the the country to and around Petersburgh, and returned to New York in April.

258. When, and under what leaders, did the battle of Cowpens occur?

Ans. On January 17, 1781. Gen. Nathaniel Greene, having succeeded Gates in the southern department, sent Gen. Daniel Morgan into South Carolina. Near the northern boundary, at Cowpens, Tarleton, under Cornwallis, met him, and a severe battle was fought, in which the British were defeated, with great loss.   In Morgan's report, he attributed his success "to the justice of our cause and gallantry of our troops."

259. What was the next important engagement?

Ans. At Guilford Court-House, N. C., on March 15, 1781.   In this battle the patriots under Greene met the enemy under Cornwallis. The Americans were repulsed, but the British were so much broken that Charles Fox, in the British House of Commons, said: "Another such victory will ruin the British army."

260. What was the last important action of the war in Georgia?

Ans. The siege of Augusta, which lasted from April 16th to June 5, 1781.   This siege was concluded by a complete surrender.   The loss to the patriots was about 40 killed and wounded, and that of the enemy much heavier, in addition to 300 prisoners.   Lieut.-Col. Henry Lee was in command.

261. What were some of the minor engagements in the South up to the time of the surrender of Augusta, June 5, 1781.

Ans. June 8th, at Charles City Court House,

Va. (an engagement was proposed by Arnold after he had burned Richmond); on February 1st, at McCowan's Fort, N. C., and at Wilmington, N. C.; on February 6th, at Shallow Ford, N. C.; on February 12th, at Bruce Cross Roads, N. C.; on February 25th, at Haw River, N. C.; on March 2d, at Clapp's Mills, N. C.; on March 6th, at Wetzel's Mills, N. C.; on April 12, at Fort Balfour, S. C.; from April 15th to the 23d, at Fort Watson, S. C.; on April 25th, at Petersburgh, Va., and at Hillsborough, N. C.; on April 27, at Osborn's, S. C.; on May 11th, at Orangeburgh, S. C.; on the 12th, at Fort Motte, S. C.; the 14th, at Nelson's Ferry, S. C.; the 15th, at Fort Granby, S. C., and on the 21st, at Silver Bluff, S. C., and Fort Galpin, Ga.

262. What must we conclude by the above showing?

Ans. That the British were very unwilling to give up their determination to separate the Colonies in the South from those in the North.

263. What was effected by the Americans between April 25th and September 8, 1781?

Ans. Greene had chased the British out of South Carolina, except in Charleston where they were covered by their fleet.

264. Where was Cornwallis at the beginning of August, 1781?

Ans. He had transferred his 7,000 men to Yorktown and vicinity.

265. What movement was made by the allied patriotic forces in the latter part of August?

Ans. Washington, learning that the French fleet could aid on the Virginia coast, at once moved with 6,000 men (4,000 of them Frenchmen, under Count Rochambeau) from the Hudson through New Jersey to the head of the Chesapeake bay.

266. How did he prevent Clinton from guessing his destination?

Ans. He wrote letters to General Greene and sent them so as to be intercepted. These letters convinced Clinton that Washington was intending an attack on New York, and the patriots were beyond Philadelphia before their movement was understood.

267. What did Clinton then do, hoping to change their course?

Ans. He sent Arnold to the New England coast. The marauders perpetrated a horrible massacre at Fort Griswold on September 6, 1781, and burned New London. This occurred almost in sight of Arnold's birthplace.

268. Of what avail was this wretched performance of Arnold's? ·

Ans. It only added infamy to infamy. With this expedition, Arnold disappears from history.

269. When was the siege of Yorktown commenced by the Americans?

Ans. On September 28, 1781. With 16,000 men in front, and the great French fleet under De Grasse closing in behind, there was no escape for the British, and Cornwallis capitulated.

270. What was the date of Cornwallis's surrender, and what did it signify?

Ans. Cornwallis surrendered October 19, 1781, and thus practically terminated the war for American Independence.

271. What was the effect upon the country?

Ans. The news reached Philadelphia at dead of night. The people were awakened by the watchman's cry: "Past two o'clock, and Cornwallis is taken." The hardships of the past were forgotten in the thought that America was free.

272. How was the autumn passed by the American army?

Ans. Intelligence of the Yorktown surrender reached General Greene, near Charleston, on the 30th of October, but he, with Wayne and

Marion, kept up their watchful guard of the enemy, who were still entrenched in Savannah and Charleston. Washington was still keeping Clinton closely confined in New York.

273. What action did the House of Commons take?

Ans. On March 4, 1782, it ordered a cessation of hostilities.

274. How was this order met by the British army?

Ans. On July 11, 1782, they evacuated Savannah, and on December 14th they also departed from Charleston.

275. When did they evacuate New York?

Ans. On November 25, 1783, soon after the final negotiations for peace were concluded.

276. When and where was a definite treaty signed?

Ans. On September 3, 1783, at Paris.

277. Where was the American camp at this time?

Ans. At Newburgh-on-the-Hudson. On November 3, 1783, the army was disbanded, and the patriots quietly returned to their homes to enjoy the blessings of the Liberty they had won.

278. What acts of Washington followed the disbanding of the army?

Ans. He met his officers in Fraunces' Tavern,

New York, on December 4, 1783, and there bade them farewell. On December 23, 1783, he went to Annapolis and resigned the commission as Commander-in-Chief, which he had received from Congress on June 16, 1775.

WASHINGTON!

Our grandest conception of manhood is embodied in this name.   Whether we think of him in his early frontier life, or as Commander-in-Chief of the Continental Army, we find in him the wisdom and courage that could turn seeming defeat into victory.   There were those engaged with him who aspired to fill his place; but in the light of History he is so transcendent, that we wonder at the audacity that essayed to rob him of his laurels.   During the more than seven years of our struggle for freedom no one discovered faint-heartedness in this sublime leader; and because he was so sublime he was able to give heart to his army, even in the darkest hours.   When the Continental Congress could only " promise to pay " for faithful services, Washington was able to quell uprisings of the soldiers which threatened to subvert the end for which they had fought.   From victories in the field we follow him to Mount Vernon, his much-loved home, where he is the grand man still.   In less than four years, when it becomes apparent that something other than the thirteen Articles of Confederation, framed in 1774, is needed to hold the new States together, George Washington is called upon to preside over that illustrious body of great men who framed the Constitution. On the 4th of March, 1789, the "Continental Congress" closed its labors and the "Federal Constitution" became the law of the new Republic. A wise hand was needed to guide the "ship of state" out into the waters where waves and storms of trouble would come, and instinctively all hearts turned to Washington, "whose good judgment and valor were only equalled by his modesty." On April 6, 1789, he was chosen the first President of these United States. We see him in imagination again leaving Mount Vernon, and we involuntarily follow him all that long way (which he takes on horseback) to New York city, then temporarily the seat of Government. There is a vivid picture in the mind, of the scene on the street gallery of the old City Hall, at the corner of Wall and Nassau Streets, where on April 30, 1789, thousands gathered to witness the Inauguration. No one more than Washington realized the importance of the occasion, and subsequent history has proved the wisdom of the Nation's choice. One term of four years having passed a second was pressed upon him, and though longing for rest, such as his home would give, he yielded to the urgency of the times; but when a third term was proposed he was constrained to refuse utterly. His Farewell Address to the American People, which appeared on September 19, 1796, is one that no intelligent lover of this country can afford to leave unread, and his advice to the Nation is wonderfully prophetic of the Nation's need and danger. The necessity of a national capital led to the purchase of a section of land ten miles square, on the Potomac river, in 1790, and Washington honored the place by laying the corner-stone for the Capitol. Bearing the name of Washington, in 1800, that city became the seat of Government. Meantime, after a short enjoyment of his home life, Washington passed away on December 14, 1799, beloved and honored by the country he loved so well.

> "So sleep the brave who sink to rest
> With all their country's honors blest."